This book belongs to

_____

Jane Goodall

By Mary Nhin

Pictures By
Yuliia Zolotova

Copyright © 2020 by Grow Grit Press LLC. All rights reserved. No part of this book may be reproduced in any form without permission in writing from the publisher. Please send bulk order requests to growgritpress@gmail.com 978-1-63731-304-6 Printed and bound in the USA. MiniMovers.tv

Hi, I'm Jane Goodall.

When I was a young girl, I had a favorite soft toy like most children. My toy wasn't a typical teddy bear, though. My toy was a chimpanzee!

I was fascinated by the animal kingdom. But my family couldn't afford to send me to college, so I had to find work.

I traveled with friends to Kenya and worked as a secretary for a renowned archaeologist and paleontologist. My boss wanted to train me to become his assistant, as a chimpanzee researcher, so he paid for me to study at the University of Cambridge.

Not many women worked in the field then. Because of this, many people doubted my success. But I was determined, and I traveled to Tanzania to study a community of chimpanzees.

I was criticized a lot, particularly for giving each chimpanzee a name, instead of a number. I did develop an emotional attachment to the animals, but my research provided groundbreaking insights into animal behavior.

I became the only human in history to be accepted into a community of chimpanzees. I saw chimpanzee behaviors never before seen by a human.

I learned that chimpanzees were extremely intelligent. They could use tools, work co-operatively and hunt other creatures. They were also socially and emotionally more developed than we had imagined, showing affection through hugs and kisses and caring for others within their community.

When I finally had to leave the chimpanzees colony, I used my knowledge and experience to set up the Jane Goodall Institute to support future research and encourage women into the field, as well as men.

It had become clear to me that conservation and the protection of our environment, including the habitats of these creatures, was vital for the future. I've dedicated my life to this work, and I hope to have inspired the next generation to continue it.

Timeline

1980 – Jane wins the World Wildlife Award
for Conservation

1993 – Jane is given the Rainforest Alliance
Champion Award

2002 – Jane is named a United Nations
Messenger of Peace

2004 – Jane was named Dame Commander of
the Most Excellent Order of the British Empire

minimovers.tv

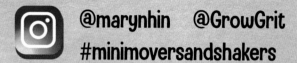 @marynhin   @GrowGrit
#minimoversandshakers

Mary Nhin   Grow Grit

Grow Grit

Manufactured by Amazon.ca
Bolton, ON

25983007R00021